Good Homes
magazine

101 colour schemes that really work!

JULIE SAVILL

Published by BBC Worldwide Ltd
Woodlands
80 Wood Lane
London W12 0TT

First published 2001
Copyright © BBC Worldwide 2001
All photographs © *BBC Good Homes* magazine 2001

ISBN 0 563 53418 4

Edited by Alison Willmott

Commissioning Editor: Vivien Bowler
Project Editor: Sarah Lavelle
Book Art Director: Lisa Pettibone
Book and Jacket Designer: Kathy Gammon
Cover Art Director: Pene Parker

Set in Amasis MT, ITC Officina Sans, New Baskerville
Printed and bound by Imprimerie Pollina, s.a.
Colour separations by Kestrel Digital Colour, Chelmsford
Jacket printed by Imprimerie Pollina, s.a.

Contents

Introduction

I t can lift you up, calm you down, set your pulse racing, even suppress your appetite. We're talking colour, and it's the most powerful tool you can use to turn the home you have into the home you want. It's also one of the most exciting stages of decorating when you get to choose the shades for a brand new scheme. Riffling through the samples, flicking through the paint companies' brochures and browsing through magazines and catalogues adds up to a totally enjoyable Sunday afternoon on the sofa!

Up close and personal

One thing's for sure, whether they're a committed hint-of-a-tint type or belong to the bright-is-right camp, everyone has a colour crisis at some point – that shade of lip-withering lemon that looked so creamy in the tin, for instance, or the sizzling combination of orange and lime that seemed like such a good idea at the time…

So how do you create those dreamy schemes that look as if they're lifted straight from the pages of a magazine? Well, first off you need to remember that colour is an intensely personal thing and the only reason for choosing a scheme should be that it pleases you and (hopefully) your family. If brown and pink does it for you, fine. If you feel happy painting

▶ If you like smart black and tailored lines, a dark scheme with strong shapes may suit you. The black leather sofa and blocks of purple on the walls are lifted by the pale carpet.

and repainting until you chance upon a combination that works, that's great too. But if you want to save yourself time and money you'll want a scheme that's right first time. A scheme, maybe, that lends a warmer feel to a chilly, dark room, or the right colours to open up a tiny space and give it an illusion of airiness. That's where this book earns its keep. From the practical advice in the first chapters to the 101 tried and tested schemes for every room in the house, it takes the sting out of decorating and will make sure you never drop another colour clanger.

▲ Small swatches of material are helpful in deciding whether colour combinations work well together.

◄ Layers of classic *toile de Jouy* fabrics in a mix of colours and a canopy of finely striped voile evoke the romance and elegance of a French château.

The colour test

Colour is nothing to be scared of and anyone can learn to use and love brighter shades with stunning effect. And, if you are a colour novice, a few words of friendly advice. Don't judge a shade by the first brushful on the wall – or even the colour of the whole wall. You will never see that full expanse of solid colour when the room is in normal use so, for the moment, turn a blind eye, move the furniture back in, get some pictures on the wall, add your favourite props and accessories and then, and only then, step back and take your first proper look at the effect. Still not convinced anything braver than beige is for you? Then consider using colour in smaller amounts, starting with cushions or vases and working up to a feature wall in a bold shade. But even if you stay rooted in the neutral palette there are creative ways to blend and contrast shades to give depth, texture and interest. But don't take my word for it; start reading…

Julie Savill
Editor, *BBC Good Homes*

Colour

Getting inspired

Making it work

basics

Changing spaces

Adding impact

Choosing colours for a room is fun but it can also be a daunting prospect. Just take a look at the mind-boggling array of paint shades on the shelves of any DIY store. Even white is not simply white – paint companies offer a range of hints and tints as well as the pure version – while a colour such as blue comes in hundreds of different shades, from cool ice to classic navy. How do you begin to choose?

Perhaps your colour choices are narrowed down by an existing feature of your room, say a carpet you like too much to change or a bathroom suite you can't afford to replace. Or you may have an accessory, such as a picture or rug, that you can use as a starting point. If it includes a mix of colours that go well together, try picking these out to use on the walls, flooring and furniture. Fabric prints can do the same trick – if you've found a design you want to use in a big way, then matching your paint shade to one of its key colours can result in a very successful scheme.

If there is no obvious starting point, and your room is a blank canvas, you have

▲ Pattern power

Striking prints make good starting points for room schemes. This pea-green wall colour was matched to a shade used in the vegetable design. Fabric prints usually feature several tones of one colour; for this room the brightest was chosen to balance the vibrancy of the lively pattern.

Getting inspired

Having a colour crisis? Learn the tricks the designers use to dream up their schemes.

the entire colour palette to choose from. You may know which shades you like – but somehow you doubt that your favourite scarlet will suit the relaxing bedroom you had in mind. Or perhaps you've never given colour much thought before. Bewildered by the vast choice, you may feel tempted just to stick a pin in a paint chart. There's a chance that this will work – but only a tiny one. If you want to be sure of coming up with a colour scheme you can love and live with, what you need is inspiration.

Finding your true colours

Colour is largely a matter of taste – what looks like luscious lime to one person is sickly green to another. So the first thing you need to do is find the colours you like best – your personal favourites. If you aren't sure what these are, then just take a look in the mirror. By applying to your home the instincts you use to colour-scheme your clothes,

▲ Neutral gear

Transferring your dress sense to your decor means focusing on both colours and patterns that you like. Earthy greens, golds and browns work as well together in this sitting room as they do in the dress and jacket that inspired the scheme.

you'll have a strong lead for the shades you'll feel happiest living with.

Open your wardrobe doors and ask yourself a few simple questions. Which colours feature most among your clothes collection? What colour do you feel most comfortable wearing? Have you got any favourite patterns or prints? Take a garment that matches each of your answers and hang them beside each other on a wall, then stand back and imagine how you could use their colours in your rooms.

The chances are that if you wear mainly pastel colours and pretty prints you'll want soft feminine shades in your home, but if punchy reds and oranges are more your thing you'll be happier with a much bolder scheme. On the other hand, you might feel that the shades that suit you best aren't necessarily the ones you'd want on your walls – or maybe your partner doesn't adore that little purple number quite as much as you do! If so, all is not lost; there is another way of discovering which colours do it for you.

If you're reading this, you probably already realize how helpful books and magazines can be. Look through all the colour schemes in the second part of this book and earmark any you like, then do the same with a few magazines. Don't

worry just yet about whether the schemes will work in your own home – just go for colours that appeal to you.

When you've tagged a sufficient selection of pages, take another look at these and see what colours they all have in common. The results might be surprising. Perhaps you were planning to play it safe with pale neutrals, but if shocking pink crops up over and over again, and seems to be a colour you respond to, then maybe you should consider finding a place for it in your scheme.

◀ **Lighten up**

A penchant for pastel-coloured clothes and flowers in the hair translates into a room full of pale, delicate blues and lilacs and pretty prints. They add up to a relaxing scheme with an unashamedly feminine feel.

▼ Blooming lovely

Flowers resting in white china inspired this bedroom
scheme, where accents of hot fuchsia pink and
deep purple bloom against a cream backdrop. The
white bedlinen, scattered with open-faced flowers,
boldly reproduces the image of flower heads in
the bowls. The dark star anise is interpreted as rich
brown furniture.

Looking for colour clues

Identifying the colours you like is the first
step towards a winning scheme. The
second is knowing how to combine them
with others. Most room schemes comprise
two or three main hues, plus additional
shades – accent colours – that are used in
smaller amounts. Understanding colour
theory will help you get the mix right, but
before you start poring over a colour wheel,
take time out to look around you for inspiration and you may turn up some interesting
and original colour combinations.

Colour is everywhere, and the smallest
details can kick-start exciting new schemes.
Nature is a rich source of fascinating
colour combinations, and sometimes you
don't even need to step outside your front
door to find them. A few sprays of your
favourite garden flowers and foliage in a
vase may have you reaching for the colour

cards, or a bowl of apples might make you realize how shades of green, red and yellow can look stunning together.

When you do venture outdoors, keep your camera close and your eyes alert to the accidents that nature, man and time can throw your way. Strolls at the seaside or in the countryside can yield unexpected inspiration. A pair of aged blue shutters opened against the rough stone walls of a cottage, a row of brightly coloured beach huts or the subtle natural tones of sand, seashells and pebbles can all trigger clever ideas for room schemes. It's all about looking at things with a fresh eye, and taking note of shades, shapes and textures.

Setting the mood

If you've found inspiration, your head may be swimming with colour ideas but bobbing among them is also a nagging question: 'What will they feel like to live with?' You're right to be wary – shades that look

▲ Natural flavour

Earthy shades and subtle textures make a room scheme based on a basket of onions and garlic. Creams and tans are the main colours, while the texture of the basket is represented by the ribbed flooring and woven coffee table. Hints of colour on the garlic skins appear as mauve and pink cushions.

▶ **Red alert**

Cut down bathroom queues with brilliant red. It stimulates a sense of urgency and motivation so will get people in and out fast!

▲ **Slinky blue**

Can't stop snacking? Use blue in your kitchen and you may find that it suppresses hunger pangs and reduces your appetite.

▼ **Sweet dreams**

Pale pink is ideal for insomniacs as its soft, warm tones gently relax and reassure. Introduce hints of soft green for the perfect balance.

fine in a small bunch of flowers may not create the atmosphere you want on large expanses of wall or carpet. Used in the wrong rooms, some can be overpowering, overstimulating or even depressing. Others can have a positive effect, by helping to lift the spirits or create a relaxing atmosphere.

There's a whole psychology to colour that has a real effect on the way we feel and live. All colours form part of an electromagnetic spectrum where each colour vibration has a different wavelength, and it's this energy that affects us both physically and emotionally – by energizing, soothing or refreshing the senses. Choose the right colours and you can create the right atmosphere in every room of your home. Use this guide to help you get in tune with your mood:

Red is a stimulating colour that sizzles with energy. Used in a bathroom or kitchen, it acts as a wake-up call to get the family moving in the morning. Give it a miss if you want a relaxing bedroom, though.

Pink is soothing, the shade of nurturing and love. These qualities come into their own in the bedroom, where pale pink creates a tranquil, reassuring atmosphere while brighter shades can spark passion.

Orange is an energizing colour that also aids digestion, so it's great for a dining room or kitchen. But, like red, it's not

recommended if you're seeking restfulness.

Yellow is sunny and welcoming and gives a boost to any social occasion, so it's spot-on for rooms where you entertain. It might be overstimulating for chill-out spaces like bedrooms, though.

Purple and lilac add an atmosphere of calm and spirituality, so work well if you want a study or sitting room where you can shrug off the stresses of the day.

Blue sharpens your mental faculties, so is another good colour for a study. It can also help to suppress hunger pangs, so give it a go in the kitchen or dining room if that diet isn't working.

Turquoise and paler shades of aqua create a feeling of well-being and harmony. They are perfect for a soothing bathroom where the whole family can relax.

Green is a harmonizing colour that can be used in any room, although too much may create a stagnant atmosphere.

White can be a difficult colour to live with as it does not absorb colour energies but reflects them all back into the room. Pale pastels are a less stark option.

Black is the opposite to white as it absorbs all colours and puts nothing back into the room. It can act as an energy barrier and be suppressing, if not depressing.

Brown is similar to black in its effects. However, its gentle tints of red and yellow can make it feel warmer and less suppressive.

Making a sample board

Before you try to turn your colour scheming ideas into reality, put them down on paper. A sample board is the tool used by professional interior designers to create a visual impression of an entire room, from paint colour to furniture to accessories, in a form that they can present to their clients for approval. Even if you've only yourself to please, making a sample board can be time well spent, preventing costly decorating mistakes. It's a lot cheaper to swap one tiny fabric swatch for another than to get your sofa re-covered. And if you're at all unsure of how to mix and match colours, it's an invaluable way of focusing your ideas and providing further inspiration.

Find a sheet of A3 paper or card to use as a base, then collect samples of all the furnishings you plan to include in your room. Pin them all to the card, and then swap them around or add others as your ideas evolve to see how different colour combinations work together. When you feel you have a complete picture of your room and are happy with the overall effect, glue everything in place and use the board as a blueprint for your scheme. Here's what to include on your board:

Paint shade cards can be picked up from DIY stores. Include colours for all the paintwork in the room – ceiling, woodwork and any furniture you plan to paint – as well as the walls.

Carpet and flooring samples are also freely available. Small pieces of wooden flooring can be useful for representing the wood tones of furniture.

Fabric swatches are usually available on demand at furnishing stores. Include larger samples for big items such as curtains and sofas, smaller ones for cushions.

Snippets of trimmings such as piping or beading are also important as they add to the character of a room.

Photos of furniture and accessories will help to give the complete picture. Take your own photos of existing features of the room, and use cuttings from magazines and brochures for pieces you plan to buy.

Materials that suggest the mood you want to create might help to inspire you further. For example, a feather might conjure up the delicate feel you want for your bedroom. Sample boards are also known as mood boards – what you're aiming for is an effect that excites and pleases you.

A scale drawing of the room will help you plan its layout. Add measurements so that you can calculate quantities for furnishings when the time comes to buy.

▶ **Swatch watch**
Gather anything from flowers to fabrics to display on your sample board. This will give you a picture of how your ideas are shaping up and help you to develop them further.

When you've got some scheming ideas that inspire you, it's time to translate them into action – and this is where understanding a little about colour theory can make all the difference between a stunning scheme and a repainting job. The colour wheel takes the guesswork out of interior design and lets you see at a glance whether your scarlet sofa will go with your green walls, or which colours you should be considering to make the best of your blue carpet.

There's no mystique about colour – it's all a question of confidence. The position of colours on the wheel in relation to one another reveals how they will work together in a room, helping you to get the mix right for the effect that you want to create. It can tell you which shades will take the chill off a cold room or freshen up a stuffy one, which colours combine easily and which will create the most striking contrasts.

Climate control

In much the same way as it affects our moods, colour can help to conjure up a more comfortable atmosphere by making a room feel warmer or cooler. Split the

Talking colour

Colour has a language all its own, which the wheel can help you to understand:

Primary colours form its three key 'spokes' – red, blue and yellow. All the other colours are a mixture of these.

Secondary colours are the three that fall midway between the primaries – purple, green and orange. Each is made by mixing its two nearest primaries.

Other colours in between the primaries and secondaries are made by mixing the two colours adjacent to them.

Tones or shades are not shown on the wheel but are made by adding black or white to colours to make them darker or lighter. Pastels have white added, while those mixed with black are often known as muted shades.

Warm colours are all those that appear on the left-hand side of the wheel – from sunny yellow through to hot pink.

Cool colours are the calmer and more subdued ones on the right-hand side of

Making it work

For fail-safe schemes, give the colour wheel a spin and get your decorating plans on a roll.

the wheel – from green to purple.

Harmonious colours are any two that lie immediately next to one another on the wheel, and are guaranteed to work well together to make a balanced room scheme.

Complementary colours are any two that lie opposite one another on the wheel, such as red and green, and will form a lively contrast when used together.

Neutrals are the 'non-colours' that do not appear on the wheel – black, brown, white and cream, plus all the beige and grey shades in between. Neutrals will mix happily with any other colour.

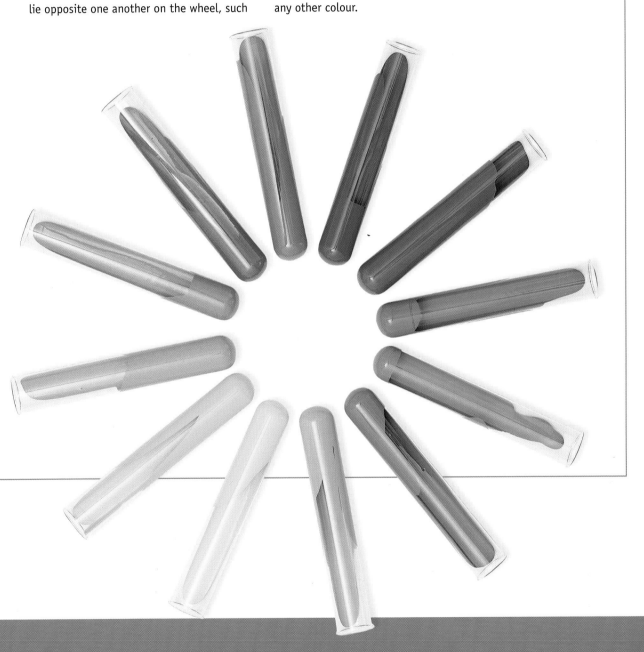

▼ Warm

Gold and orange give this bedroom a warm, sunny feel.
Deep brown furniture ensures a good tonal balance,
while fresh white bedlinen lightens things up.

► Warmer

Deep orange on the walls revs up the heat even
further. Losing the tonal balance between the walls
and the curtains makes the room more enclosed,
creating a cocoon of warmth.

wheel in half down the middle, then take
a look at the colours on the left-hand side.
Think what adjectives you might use to
describe them – sunny yellow, flaming
orange, hot pink – and you'll realize why
these are called warm colours.

If the heating's on full and the sun's out
but your room still feels bleak and cold,
what it needs is an injection of warm
colour to take off the chill. Although these
colours can't actually raise the temperature,
they will create a cosier atmosphere. Warm
colours may seem too intense in a small
space, but can make a large room feel more

inviting without overwhelming it. North-
facing rooms in particular may benefit from
a scheme based on these shades.

While warm hues appear to advance
towards you, the more subdued colours on
the cool side of the wheel – blues, greens
and purple – appear to recede, so have
the effect of making a space seem larger.
If your room feels cramped or stuffy,
decorating with these colours can help to
freshen it up. They are best used in south-
facing rooms that get plenty of natural
daylight, where there is less risk of them
adding a chilly feel.

▲ Cool

Cool blues and lilacs in different tones combine to create a relaxing bedroom scheme. The bed is bathed in daylight, offsetting any chilling effect the scheme might have.

◀ Cooler

Using paler tones of blue and lilac for the walls and curtains and adding a light bedcover alongside the other white furnishings has given the room a fresher, more spacious feel.

▶ Balancing act

Red and purple, close neighbours on the colour wheel, are watered down to soft raspberry and plum for a warm, harmonious scheme. White walls lighten the look, while a purple band adds colour. The dark shelving, red rug and pale floor cushion provide tonal variation.

▼ Perfect harmony

Harmonious colours blue and green are a cool and soothing mix. Use them in their pure form or in lighter tones on walls for an easy-to-live-with look.

Getting the mix right

When you've decided which colours will make your room feel comfortable, think about how you want to use them. If you're after a balanced look that's easy on the eye, one way of guaranteeing success is to choose two harmonious colours – that is, any two that lie next to each other on the colour wheel. They make perfect room-mates, a compatible, non-clashing combination. Using a series of harmonious shades throughout your home is also a good way of ensuring that the colour flows smoothly from room to room, with no unsightly clashes when doors are left open.

If you fancy being more adventurous, and want a dramatic contrast within a room, your best bet is to choose two complementary colours – that is, any two that lie on opposite sides of the colour wheel. These intensify each other when used together, injecting life into a scheme. The second colour is best used in small quantities – two powerful colours used in equal amounts might fight with one another.

Whether you opt for contrast or coordination, it is vital to include a range of tones – darker, mid-tone and lighter shades of your chosen colours – to prevent your scheme looking either too

Soft touch

Complementary colour can soften as well as intensify. The lilac vase takes the edge off the yellow, creating a two-tone bedroom that's easier to live with.

Opposites attract

The bright orange of the throw complements deep blue, its opposite number on the colour wheel, to give this living room an injection of energy.

Sharp contrast

A red cushion adds a dash of complementary colour to bring out the sharpness of the greens and give this scheme a touch of warmth.

washed-out and bland or dark and depressing. If your colour mix isn't working, a lack of different tones could be the culprit, while a scheme with good tonal variation is sure to succeed, even if all the shades are of one colour. To get a feel for how this works, take a look at one strip of paint shade samples from a DIY store. If you aren't sure how to use

different tones together, choose the lightest for the walls, a mid tone for the flooring, and then add darker furnishings.

Tricks of the light

Remember that colours can be affected by light. Strong tones that look dramatic by day might seem gloomy under artificial evening light. Or pastels that are soft and subtle by candlelight can appear insipid in natural daylight. For this reason it is important to test your paint shades before investing in large cans. Buy test pots and apply the colour over as large an area of your wall as possible. Then live with it for a week or two, noting how it feels in different lights. It's also a good idea to buy a metre of any fabric you like and to see if you can get hold of a larger carpet sample rather than basing your decisions on tiny swatches. When you've confirmed that it all looks great together, you can start decorating with confidence.

▲ Striking the right tone

A strip of paint shades is a handy reference tool for getting all-important tonal variation into your room. For foolproof colour scheming, simply pick a paint shade, then include other tones from the same strip in your scheme. This trick works particularly well with blues.

◀ Shades of difference

What could be simpler than using just one colour throughout your home? All you have to do to make it work is vary its tonal values. If you love yellow, start with the boldest shade you can find, then use mid-tone and paler shades in other rooms.

As far as living space goes, size matters. But before you take a sledgehammer to the walls of your poky rooms or get busy with screens and partitions to cosy up a large area, just consider what colour can do for you. By using it to trick the eye, you can create the illusion of space in a tiny room or make a huge shell seem smaller and cosier. Paint a room in white or a light pastel and it will open it up, making it feel lighter and brighter. Slap a coat of dark red on to the same walls and they will appear to close in.

The secret of changing apparent size and shape with colour lies not only in the shades you choose but also in the way you use them. Stripes and bands of colour are handy tools for making a room look taller or wider, while simply painting a ceiling in a lighter or darker shade can appear to raise or lower it. The colour of the flooring you choose will also affect the perceived proportions of your room.

Colour choices should not be governed by hard-and-fast rules; midnight blue might well look fab in a minuscule bathroom, despite its possible cramping effect. But it helps to be aware of the

▲ The basic scheme

With pale wood flooring, walls in a contemporary shade of turquoise and traditional white on the ceiling, this room looks light and modern, an ideal space for informal everyday dining. However, it would seem a little cold for an intimate dinner party or a romantic supper.

▶ Let's get friendly

For a more intimate atmosphere, all that's needed is to change the white ceiling to a rich natural. Although the turquoise on the walls is a cool colour, it is inviting enough to adapt to the cosier mood. The room appears smaller but retains its modern feel.

Changing spaces

Rooms too tall, too wide, too small? See how colour can transform their apparent size and shape.

▲ The basic scheme

▶ Space ace

Painting a band of lighter blue directly under the
cornice makes the room seem larger, creating a
two-fold effect. By drawing the eye upward, it
appears to lift the ceiling and defines the contours
of the room. Also, by creating a horizontal line
around the walls, it makes the space look wider.

▼ Feel the width

Using a lighter colour above dado level opens the
walls out, making the room seem wider, while
repeating the turquoise of the lower walls on the
ceiling exaggerates this effect. Painting the ceiling
a deep colour appears to lower it, so compromise
with a paler shade in low rooms.

illusions colour can create, and to understand how, if you feel your rooms are too big, too narrow, too small or too tall, a can of paint can provide an easy cure.

Making it bigger

If you want to give the impression of space, opt for pale colours. Those that work best are neutrals such as cream or white or very light tones of hues from the cool side of the colour wheel, such as blues and greens. Cool colours appear to recede, so have the effect of opening up a small room. For maximum effect, paint all the walls and the ceiling in the same light shade, and fit pale flooring. Paint features such as radiators and fitted cupboards in the same colour as the walls so that they blend in. If you want to use a deeper shade on the walls, choose a cool colour, and stick to white for the ceiling to make the room seem light and lofty.

Reflective surfaces are also good at adding to the illusion of space. Mirrors are invaluable – a large wall mirror that reflects most of a small room can appear to double its size. Shiny or transparent surfaces such as stainless steel, chrome, glass and Perspex are also helpful because they reflect light.

Making it cosier

To give a large space a more intimate atmosphere, choose a warm wall colour, such as red, orange or yellow. If you prefer a colour from the cool side of the spectrum, choose a deep rather than a pale shade. Warm colours appear to advance

▲ The basic scheme

With pale wood flooring and cream walls, this sitting room looks light and spacious. But with no colour to warm it up, the scheme makes the high-ceilinged room feels chilly. It also appears featureless – the fireplace almost vanishes when it's a similar colour to the walls.

▶ Getting hotter

If you want to make a room feel more inviting, paint just one feature wall in a warm colour. Orange adds impact and defines the fireplace. It also makes the far wall appear closer, so the room looks a little smaller.

towards you so be prepared for them to make the room feel smaller as well as cosier. Replacing light flooring with a darker shade will also make the space shrink. Consider how it will affect your wall colour – a blue carpet makes cream walls seem colder, while a red will warm them up.

Altering its shape

If your room is too tall rather than too large, painting the ceiling in a colour or a rich neutral instead of white will make it seem lower. Continuing the colour down on to the coving and around the tops of the walls will increase this effect. In the

same way, if you have a long, narrow room, painting one end wall in a strong, warm colour will appear to draw it towards you, making the room seem shorter.

Striped walls are also good at correcting shape problems. To make a low-ceilinged room look taller, try vertical

▲ Floor show

Replacing the light flooring with a dark-toned carpet makes the room feel smaller and more cosy. But watch out – a darker flooring can also affect the wall colour. Here, the cream walls reflect the blue of the carpet, which makes them look colder.

▼ Raising the roof

Painting the walls in coordinating vertical stripes draws the eye upwards, adding the illusion of height to make this bedroom seem taller. It also adds an element of pattern and interest to the scheme.

stripes in coordinating colours. The narrower the stripe, the greater the effect. To make a room seem wider, use horizontal stripes. Painting them along one wall only should do the trick, but don't try this unless your home has high ceilings as it will make them appear lower.

▼ **Pale and uninteresting**

Pale neutrals are a foolproof if undaring choice.
A two-tone natural scheme in cream and white
is a hardy perennial, but lacks emotional punch
without a contrasting third colour to warm it up.

▶ **Grand entrance**

Painting the door denim blue transforms the safe
but dull neutrals, adding instant drama. An added
bonus is that when you get bored with the scheme,
the door is the only feature you need to redecorate!

You've found a colour combination you like, you've included a range of dark and light tones, but you can't help feeling that your scheme looks a little flat. If this sounds familiar, then try a few tricks of the interior designer's trade to give it a lift. There's no need to go back to the drawing board and replan your whole room – it can be as simple as introducing a coloured vase or a few patterned cushions.

Using accent colours

Think of a colour scheme and the chances are you'll come up with a two-tone answer. Green or blue with cream, or taupe with white, are all tried and tested favourites, but add a dash of a third colour and they double their appeal. Just a little splash or stripe of another hue – known as an accent colour – can make all the difference to your scheme, adding visual excitement by contrasting with the principal shades.

Use accent colours in small amounts – to pick out window frames, a dado rail or a skirting board. They are great design tools as you can use them to create a focal point in an otherwise featureless room; the

Adding impact

Give your schemes the edge with prints, patterns
or a dash of contrasting colour.

▶ Snow white

When it comes to highlighting features, most people play it safe and pick them out in white. Used on this fire surround, it provides a contrast with the taupe shade on the walls but the overall effect is rather cold and functional.

▼ Go for glow

A coat of scarlet paint adds character to the fireplace, endowing it with the cosy glow it needs and giving it increased impact as a focal point. It also brings out the warmth in the taupe background.

plainest door will get itself noticed when painted in a bold or bright shade. Accents can also help to emphasize any interesting features you do have – highlighting a fireplace or alcove with colour will lend it additional impact.

Complementary colours work particularly well as accents. Find the main shade of your scheme on the colour wheel and its complement is the colour directly opposite. For example, a blue scheme would be enhanced by orange. Another way of choosing accents is to pick out colours that appear in a small way in a noticeable feature of the room – a picture or rug, for example.

If your room is decorated mainly in light neutrals or soft hues, go for a bold or bright accent that contrasts with them and livens up the look. In a more boldly decorated room, look for accents that are strong enough to balance the main colour – such as dashes of black or navy against a red background – or choose a light but bright contrast such as white or yellow.

If you're not sure whether a certain colour will work, put aside your paintbrush and pick up a few colourful accessories instead. Throws, cushions, vases and lamp-shades are all great ways of adding accents, and can easily be changed if you don't like the effect or fancy giving your scheme a new look. Just make sure you use accent colour sparingly, confining it to smaller accessories or specific features of the room – overdo it, and it won't be an accent!

◀ Green routine

The pale tones of gently warmed cream and sage green create a soothing atmosphere for a living room that is elegantly subtle. But the white woodwork, although toning with the cream, does little to enhance the scheme.

▲ Plum job

A touch of plum on the window frame and skirting board complements the soft green of the walls and lifts the whole look, making the room feel warmer and more welcoming.

Using patterns

Many successful schemes are created using nothing but plains, but elements of pattern can bring an extra dimension to a room. Patterns and prints have movement; they can add pace by livening up a roomful of flat neutrals or soothe and slow down the rhythm by breaking up blocks of bold colour.

The easiest way to start using pattern in a room is with soft furnishings, keeping the walls relatively plain. Collect a number of fabric samples that might go with the colours of your paintwork and flooring – look for ones that are similar in colour or tone. If you want to mix patterns, don't overdo it with one type but choose a selection of stripes, checks and other prints such as florals.

Pick a pattern

Checks and stripes are the classics of the pattern world – they can be low-key and casual, or regimental and smart. When combining more than one design, vary the sizes of the checks and stripes, and include some plains for a livable look.

Florals don't have to be old-fashioned and chintzy. Today's contemporary patterns will work well in most settings, from lively living rooms to pretty bedrooms. Choose one large-scale flower print, then add to it with a couple of smaller bud or sprig designs. Include plain fabrics and crisp modern ginghams to give your scheme an up-to-date edge.

Abstract or geometric prints, such as curvy organic shapes and retro-style blocks and circles, can be used to add movement to a scheme while underlining its modern character.

Texture can introduce pattern on a subtle scale, and is particularly useful for adding interest to a neutral scheme. Wicker furniture, fake fur cushions, ribbed sofa covers and knitted throws all add an element of pattern without being overpowering.

Coordinated collections of furnishings produced by fabric houses offer an easy option, but can give too contrived a look if used throughout a room. For a more individualistic mix, choose prints that have different designs but are similar in colour or tone.

◀ Cream team

Prints in one colour plus cream bring eye-catching detail to this sitting room without overpowering its soothing neutrals. The taupe and cream design of the sofa cover adds subtle interest over a large area. Bolder pattern is added in smaller amounts with the checked throw and the cushion covers.

▲ Lilac link

A bed offers plenty of scope for making pattern the focal point of a room, so be creative with cushions, covers and pillowcases. The starting point here was the strong lilac stripe on the duvet cover, a shade that is repeated on the walls and in many of the prints. Using it as a link colour allows a successful mix of many different designs and fabrics – from chintz to Indian silks.

Keep scale in mind, and limit yourself to one large design, making up the rest with smaller, complementary patterns. Large prints or busy patterns can look dramatic but tend to dominate a scheme. A highly patterned carpet or sofa might need to be calmed down with plains and stripes. If you like a large print but don't want it to take over your room, use it on a smaller item such as an armchair or footstool. Take care with tiny prints too – used in abundance, they can make a large room feel empty or a small room look twee. If you use a small print on walls or other big areas, mix it with larger patterns in cushions and throws.

One subtle way of adding interest to a plain scheme is to choose prints that incorporate just two colours. Keep one colour the same throughout; for example, if cream is your common colour, look for prints that each combine it with one other hue, choosing a limited palette of shades that are close in tone. Prints in one colour plus cream can be as calming and easy on the eye as plains. To add a subtle dash of pattern, use these simple tonal designs in moderation – to cover a piece of furniture or to paper just one wall in a room.

If you want to go to town with pattern a bit more, start by setting the scene with one key colour, which will probably be the shade you paint your walls. Use this as your link colour, making sure that most of the patterns you choose contain at least a little of it. You can then have fun with a mixture of bold and subtle prints in different styles and fabrics for an interesting, eclectic look.

Colour

Sitting rooms · Kitchens · Dining

schemes

rooms   Bedrooms   Bathrooms

▶ Combine a range of shades
– from deep, dark plums to
damson reds – to create an
air of decadent comfort. Soft
purples and reds bring a
luxurious feel to a sitting room.
You may find plum too strong
as a wall colour, but when used
for the plaid chair cover and
curtains, it warms up the room.
Cream cushions add the
finishing touch.

Sitting rooms

▲ Warm and cool colours blend beautifully in this room, with walls painted in a muted mid-toned aqua forming a tranquil backdrop for sumptuous shades of hot pink. Look for luxurious curtain and cushion fabrics in dusky plums and purples, but keep furniture simple for a subtle contemporary feel. Frosted-glass surfaces have a light but sophisticated look. Accents of leaf green in cushions and smaller accessories add a hint of freshness.

▶ A ripple of raspberry pink will give you a classy but cosy sitting room. Combine it with cream or white and you can't go far wrong – use it on the walls for maximum warmth, then team with a light carpet and furnishings. Add elements of pink to the curtains and furniture: make a cover for a table, pile sofas with cushions, and stitch on coloured bands to give curtains a stronger look. Chic stripes are a classic touch, and pretty chintzy florals evoke a comforting country feel.

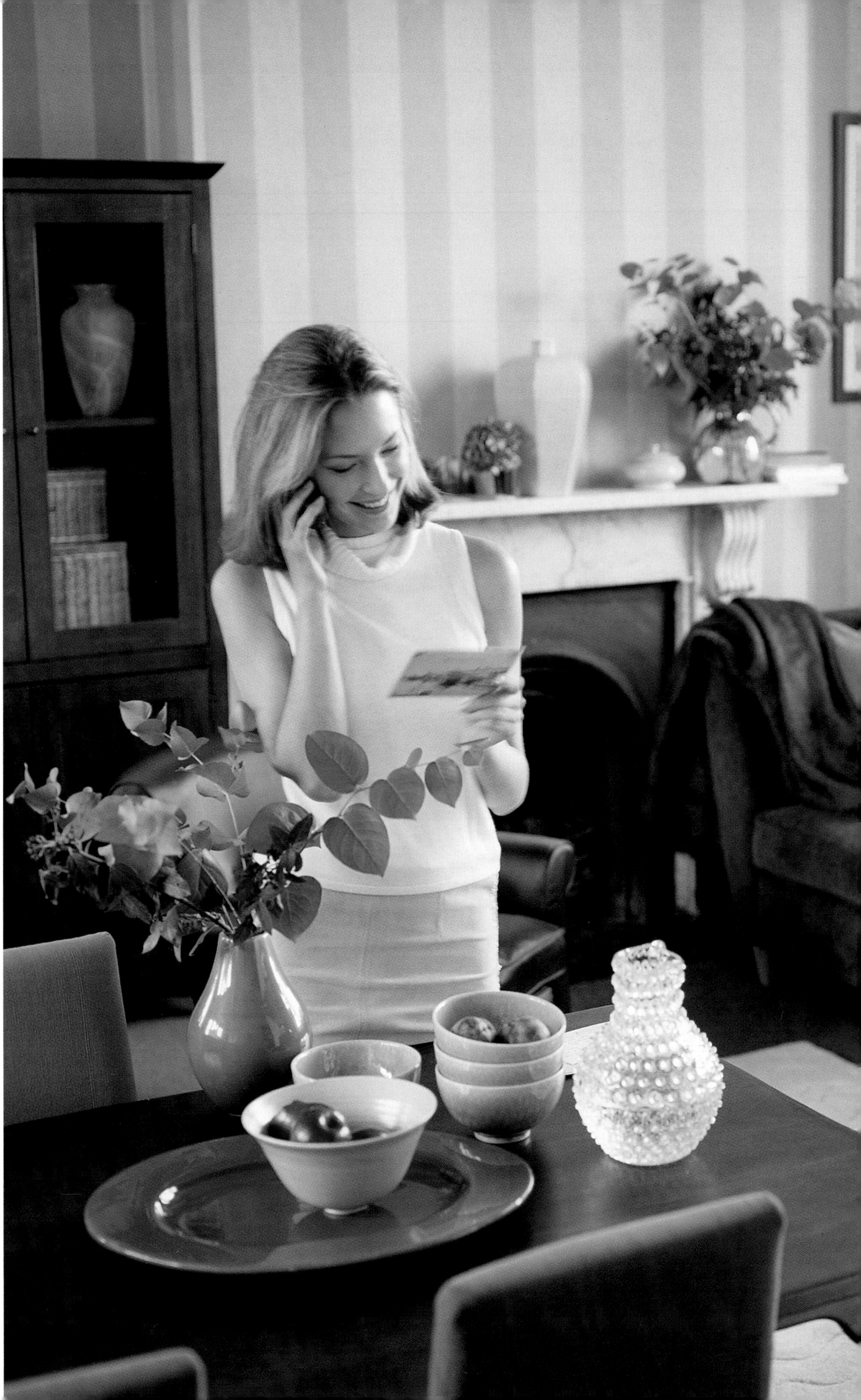

▲ Balls of knitting wool lined up in a department store provided the colour feast that inspired this relaxing sitting room scheme. Aubergine and purple nestle happily alongside subtle shades of aqua in the two-toned vertically striped wallpaper and the grey-tinged carpet. Soft textures reflect the touch-me feel of the wool. Dark wood furniture blends with the moody quality of the colours, while a few white accents are enough to give the look a lift.

◀ If you're torn between an invigorating and a relaxing feel for your sitting room, then compromise with zesty lemon yellow on the walls and cool mauve furnishings to mellow the mood. This bright contemporary scheme includes a range of mauve shades, from the pale lavender carpet to the lilac-painted table to deep purple accents in the bold checked curtains, which also feature yellow to unite the two main colours of the room.

▲ Purple and silver is a combination that spells contemporary chic. The skirting and shelf system were painted in white to provide a fresh contrast to the purple walls, then touches of silver were added with accessories such as the galvanized metal boxes and tealight holder. The sofa is layered with soft-textured throws and cushions in colours that harmonize with the purple – a range of tones from pale blue to bright pink and turquoise.

▲ The weathered timber of sun-bleached shutters open against an old stone wall sparked the idea for this soothing scheme. Decorating with natural tones and textures can be too predictable, but using soft blue as a background colour lifts the overall look. Include a few different shades of blue to give depth. Reinforce the sense of stone with textured accessories such as the woven floor cushion and the rugged bouclé of the sofa cover.

▶ For a real summery feel, pick blues that pack a punch. Mixing different shades of blue is a decorator's trick that works every time. Choose a mid-tone for the walls and a deep shade as an accent colour – in this room the indigo footstool, cushion and throw fit the bill. Add plenty of creamy white and light neutrals to lift the scheme, and include some pattern to perk up the plains. Smart checks and stripes work best with this fresh look.

◀ Harmonizing blues and lilacs mixed with a generous dollop of creamy white create a beautifully tranquil scheme. The key to putting together a relaxing look is to use mainly muted shades, such as the powdery blue on the walls and the soft lilac of the floor runner and cushions. The stronger mauve of the sofa and the darker blue of the checked armchair add tonal variation, while a touch of spring freshness comes from light green accents.

▲ Simple checks and stripes form the basis of this smart blue and white scheme. The back wall is painted in four different shades of blue in adjacent squares to make a backdrop of big checks – a striking effect when used on just one or two walls. Soft furnishings in clean-cut navy and white stripes make for a crisp look, which is softened by accents of small floral sprigs. Used in small amounts, they don't detract from the bold geometry.

▶For an airy Scandinavian feel, mix
a palette of beautiful blues, from palest
duck-egg to classic navy, and combine them
with plenty of crisp white to keep the look
light. The combination of stripes and checks
brings pace to the scheme, the vertical wall
stripes giving the room the illusion of height.
Simple whitewashed furniture reinforces the
Scandinavian theme, the curvy scalloped edge
of the table softening the regimented effect
of the checks and stripes.

Sitting rooms

◀ If you've played it safe with go-with-any-thing upholstery, the world of colour is wide open to you. In a sun-drenched room, temper the heat with a mid-tone blue that's as refreshing as a dip in the sea. Hot accents of orange, red and yellow in the cushions and picture help to intensify the coolness of the blue, while furniture, flooring and accessories in a range of warm wood tones prevent the overall effect from taking on too chilly a feel.

▲ Lilac and turquoise is a cool combination, but add some bright red and it immediately takes on a more powerful character. The quirky tartan rug and the big scarlet blooms on the cushions cut through the sweetness of the scheme. They also add some welcome pattern among the clean blocks of plain colour which, although space-enhancing, can be dull on their own. The natural wood of the simple shutters glows warmly against the cool lilac walls.

▲ Bring together green and tangerine, then stand back and watch them sizzle. Getting the balance right is important: use green on just one wall and introduce liberal amounts of crisp white to temper the overall effect. The blue curtains help to cool things down, while adding a panel of darker colour to relieve the expanse of white. The woven texture of the sofa gives the room a tropical feel, enhanced by the huge palm and the bamboo shelf unit.

▶ Keep that carefree holiday feel all year round with a vibrant, modern scheme based on the colours of a summer beach. The deep blue of a cloudless sky covers the walls, while a sun-bleached driftwood effect is suggested by the pale upholstery of the sofa, the rough, unfinished wood of the furniture and the twiggy lampbase. Glowing rainbow hues add accent colour in the shape of sheer linen window panels and brightly striped cushions.

◀ You can't go wrong with green, the colour of nature. Take a look outdoors and you'll see how it goes with everything – a great little mixer. For a sitting room that's both relaxing and refreshing, combine plain painted walls with simple leaf and flower patterns for the sofa cover and other soft furnishings. The wood grain of floorboards and chair enhances the natural theme to complete a scheme that's contemporary but with more than a hint of country charm.

▲ Bold squares in several shades of green bring the fresh feel of summer foliage indoors. Apple, lime and salad shades spar with verdant grassy greens, while the sage-coloured sofa introduces a more sober note. Flowing fern patterns continue the leafy theme onto the cushions and upholstery, working with the curves of the furniture to soften the effect of the geometric wall scheme. The sheer curtain panel, white woodwork and glass accessories keep the look crisp.

▲ The smallest details can inspire original schemes. A bundle of elastic bands in light, energizing colours was the cue for this contemporary sitting room, where yellow walls complement the strong orange of the curtains. The white floorboards and table keep the look fresh, while the off-white sofa and pale grey desk give it a little more depth. The lines of the elastic bands are reflected in the striped patterns of the curtains and picture.

▲ Go for glamour with glittering golds. Shimmering organza and reflective silks add a glint to soft furnishings, while the wall is accented with strips of gold paper. Don't over-do the Midas touch, though, or your room could end up looking more brass tacks than gold standard. Balance glitzy items with softer textures and complementary neutrals – the light-coloured silk cushions are highlighted against the rich conker brown of the sofa.

▶ A sofa covered in navy pinstripe wool sets the tone for a scheme that looks as smart as a neatly tailored suit. A backdrop of yellowy creams, camels and light wood furniture softens its air of dark formality for a look that's calming and comfortable. A checked design in broken white lines was added to one wall to resemble tailor's chalk. Subtle texture comes from the corduroy curtains and the bouclé fabric used to cover the coffee table.

◀ Neutrals are the quiet classics of interiors – choose a beige or cream suite, carpet and curtains and you can combine them with any colours you choose. Or why not go all the way with neutrals and use them throughout your room? The simplest way to coordinate beige basics is to paint the walls a shade or two darker, then carry through the neutral theme with tans, chocolates and caramels in cushions and throws. Add depth with texture – nubbly fabrics and rattan furniture.

▲ Bland magnolia gave neutrals a bad name, but with the right blend of coffee, cream and chocolate you can whisk up a very tasteful scheme. The trick is to mix different shades, from white and beige through to tan and dark browns. If you don't want to go overboard with pattern, add interest with subtle two-tone designs or touchy-feely textures – wicker, knitted cushions, a bobbly throw. To really bring the look to life, add accents in one strong colour, such as a sharp leafy green.

▲ A rugged leather sofa can look as much at home in a light, modern sitting room as in a darkly traditional setting. A delicate lilac on the walls and a stylish floral print in toning shades give a colourful lift to the sombre brown leather, while the glowing wood floor reflects its warm quality. Adding a pale-coloured rug keeps the overall effect light. For a softer, romantic look, you could try mixing leather with smaller florals in subtle pastel shades.

▶ Mellow yellows complement the warm rustic tones of wooden furniture and flooring to create a laid-back living room. The cream sofa keeps the look light, while fresh contemporary checks in blue and brick-red enliven and update the comfortable country feel. Plain-coloured bowls and vases with simple lines also add a modern edge, while textured furnishings such as the wicker chair and jute fringing on the cushions play along with the rustic influence.

▲ For year-round sunshine, paint your sitting room in bright yellow. In a sparsely furnished contemporary scheme, it adds instant warmth, bringing a Mediterranean glow to the walls. The clean lines and curves of the furniture define the modern mood, while wicker and wood boost the comfort factor. The fireplace is picked out in white as a focal point, and the striped rug and spotted cushion add simple pattern.

▲ If you want to boost the snuggle factor in your sitting room, decorate in a spectrum of deliciously warm colours. The buttery yellow on the walls makes the most of the natural light that floods in through the large window, while the big sofas are just made to sink into, the velvety texture of the upholstery making their glowing colours all the more inviting. Honey-toned wood blends beautifully with the orange and plum shades.

▲ Take the road to Marrakesh with pungent spicy colours, comfy low seating and a softly tented ceiling for a Moroccan-style scheme. Fiery shades of terracotta, saffron and red will bring a blast of Sahara sun to the chilliest room. Use them in cushions and throws piled on sofas, or in floor cushions that enable you to sit at your low table, choosing colourful stripes and exotic fabrics. To really rock the kasbah, add fretwork screens, carved wooden furniture and gold candle lanterns.

▶ Paint just one feature wall in a deep, warm colour and it's almost guaranteed to make your whole room feel cosier and more inviting. The other walls in this room are painted in a fresh yellow, as seen reflected in the mirror. Both colours tone with the wooden flooring and furniture, while the cream-coloured armchair adds a lighter touch. The rich Regency red provides a fittingly traditional backdrop for the original fireplace and ornate golden mirror frame.

76

▶ Take your kitchen down Mexico way, with hot pinks and guacamole green on walls and shelving. If you don't want to overdo the sizzling style, choose cooling blues for units and worktops, and clean, white, splashback tiles. Silvery-grey floor tiles and metal appliances boost the Mexican wave, but much of the action comes from accessories, such as punched tin frames and painted pottery.

Kitchens

▶ Team cool tonal colours and sharp lines with chrome, glass and rubber for a clinical-style kitchen, the ultimate in clean living. Panels of smoky blues and greys on the walls create a relaxing feel – for an easy-clean finish use a grime- and moisture-resistant emulsion specially designed for kitchens. Pale blue glitter flooring adds an unexpected touch of fantasy. The ice-white units have been left without kickboards to mimic freestanding style.

△ If you're going to paint your units, why not have fun with colour and do them in several shades? This idea works best in larger kitchens where it adds interest to long banks of cupboards. Here a selection of blues and aquas covers the doors and drawers, and is repeated on the insides of open storage cubes on the wall. Cork flooring provides warmth underfoot, while a galvanized metal splashback and shiny accessories bring out the steely quality of the blues.

▲ When warmed up with reds and pinks,
blue springs to life. In this kitchen the
ice-cool shade used on both the walls and
worktops has been teamed with cherry red
to evoke a retro fifties feel in a contemporary
setting, the chequerboard floor adding pattern
with pace. Steel runs through the kitchen as
a theme, lending it an industrial feel while
also reflecting light and emphasizing the
coolness of the blue. The brown wood of the
drawers softens the overall look.

◀ A fresh scheme of blue and cream strikes the right style note in this kitchen, the design of which was inspired by the retro-look dresser. The units were overhauled to match its fifties style, then they and the dresser were all given a coat or two of pale blue paint. Cream walls provide a balanced backdrop, and both colours come together in the rubber floor tiles, laid in a chequerboard pattern. Smart steel handles and accessories keep the look cool.

▲ Blue is a very popular choice for kitchens, but if you want a more individual look lavender is a colourful but relaxing alternative. This contemporary favourite is great for updating old units or adding a touch of class to plain ones. In this kitchen it is combined with cream tiles, which provide a light contrast. An oak table and chairs and wooden worktops add warmth, while deeper blue, red and purple accents give more depth to the scheme.

▶ An intriguing combination of steel and stone characterizes this kitchen. Units revamped with steel cladding and smart modern handles give an industrial feel, while the weathered stone floor tiles and luxurious marble splashback add texture to the scheme. An ugly boiler was boxed in with panels of per-forated steel. A colourwash in a Mediterranean blue takes the chill off the room, aided by the warm tones of the beech worktops.

▲ Midnight blue is a good choice for a kitchen that's also used for evening entertaining, and painting the wall units the same colour helps them to fade into the background. A touch of warmth comes from the vibrant tangerine of the neighbouring room, which shines through the doorway to prevent the dark blue from becoming too oppressive. Colourful mugs, jugs and bowls on the shelves and a collection of utensils hanging from pegs add further relief.

▲ Recreate French farmhouse style with an
old wooden table and chairs, corn-yellow walls
and units in a deep lavender blue. It all adds
up to a look that brings indoors the heady
sun-drenched feel of summer fields. Use colour
to reinvent boring units but leave natural
wood furnishings as they are – the open wall
unit and old-fashioned plate rack make good
display spaces for brightly coloured pottery.
Big, bold wall tiles unite the blue and yellow.

◀ Sharply contrasting blue and orange jostle together for a look that is lively and uplifting. They team so well because they are complementary colours, but the key to using two vibrant hues like this is to ensure that one dominates – in this case orange leads the way to create a truly high-energy atmosphere. Pace and pattern come from the bold retro-style circles on the tiles, while accessories in blue and orange take the colour theme all the way.

▲ A dolly-mixture assortment of tiles brings show-stopping colour to this splashback, adding a bright and cheerful feel to a family kitchen. The starting point for the scheme was the pale blue fridge; the tiles include both pale and darker blues, which are teamed with complementary oranges to intensify the shot of colour. The darkest of the blues was chosen to paint the walls, a deep cornflower shade that enriches the vibrancy of the tiles.

▲ Refreshing lime green walls and pale birch units and worktops help to create the illusion of space in this narrow kitchen, while aluminium splashbacks reflect light. Bold blue and white in geometric patterns – the striped blind and chequerboard flooring – sharpen up the look. Behind the hob, the white mosaic splashback with its scattering of blue and grey tiles breaks up the expanse of aluminium to make a feature of the cooking area.

▶ For an understated modern-country look, choose panelled units in cream rather than a natural wood finish. Here they create a predominantly light atmosphere in a narrow galley kitchen, with rustic terracotta-style floor tiles adding a touch of warmth. Splashback tiles in a selection of vivid shades inject a shot of bright colour. Arranged in stripes that run all the way along the wall, they make a dramatic feature of the kitchen's length.

◀ Cook up a look with a slightly fifties flavour by painting your units in mint green and adding cool, pistachio-coloured worktops. Sticking with the retro idea, a soft yellow laminate serves as a splashback. The walls also got a lick of light yellow, while beechwood flooring and a rattan chair add a relaxed, natural feel. The update of the units was completed with slick steel handles, and matching pans and appliances bring a gleam to the worktops.

▲ Cool light green has a space-enhancing effect on a small kitchen, especially when used to cover the entire wall surface. This fresh but muted tone is easier on the eye and more relaxing than a sharper citrus shade. Its natural quality complements the wood-effect vinyl flooring and birch veneer units, while its coolness tones with the stainless steel cooker hood and other metal fittings, adding a slick modern edge to the scheme.

◀ The inspiration behind this kitchen scheme was a pottery jug featuring the blues and yellows of the Spanish-style splashback tiles. Washing the walls above in a sunny yellow enhances the Mediterranean atmosphere. The beech worktops, the pine stools and the woven baskets that provide storage beneath the island unit add a faintly rustic feel, while the simply styled units in a soft shade of cream keep the overall look light and contemporary.

▲ Get in harmony with greyed-off shades of blue and green which are just right for a kitchen with a modern country feel. The simple Shaker-style units are painted in a light aquamarine and topped with a plain cream worktop. A patchwork of splashback tiles in a mixture of sage, palest green and watery blue underlines the country atmosphere. The walls are painted in a bright yellow which warms up the room without dominating it.

▲ Pine-forest green carries with it a suggestion of the great outdoors and country style, without being openly rustic. Gold-coloured door and drawer knobs add an elegant touch against the dark units. The dazzling white tiles provide a light contrast to alleviate the heaviness of the green, but are peppered with small inset tiles to bring the two colours together and prevent too stark a division between the wall and base units. The worktops are in a softer cream.

If you love the warmth and patterning of wood grain, oak is a classic choice for a kitchen. With their unfussy panelling and simple white knobs, these solid-framed units are plain enough to suit a contemporary setting but also look perfectly at home alongside the old wooden dresser. Wall-to-wall yellow – in the vivid paint shade and checked window blind – makes the most of the rich wood tones to create a scheme that simply glows with warmth.

▲ Earthy terracottas and a glowing melon-yellow on the walls combine to bring a blast of Mediterranean sunshine to this small kitchen. Simple Shaker-style birch units with a light beech worktop keep the look light and unfussy. The big splashback tiles in shades of terracotta and sand have a mottled, weathered look that enhances the sun-baked feel of the room. At the window, a Roman blind in an orange and yellow check echoes the tile colours.

▶ Warm tones of orange add a sociable, positive energy to a kitchen. Brighter citrus-style shades may be too startling of a morning but a softer orange like this will ease you more gently into the day. For maximum effect, use it on both walls and units. Keep the warm tones coming with natural wooden flooring and furniture and creamy tiles with that handmade look. Wooden serving platters and terracotta tableware complement this scheme.

▲ The glowing tones of cherrywood units set the mood for this kitchen, which fuses warmth with modern good looks. Their orangey hue is picked up by the window blind, and the colours in its design are in turn repeated in the pinks, blues and greens of the multicoloured splashback tiles. Stainless steel appliances add gleaming finishing touches, echoing the handles of the units. The walls and ceiling are painted in cream and white to offset the brighter colours.

▲ If you've a zest for colour, try setting
your kitchen on fire with a tangy, deep-toned
orange. Using it on the walls should provide
more than enough heat, so cool down the
atmosphere with pale blue, which here
enhances the quiet simplicity of the Shaker-
style units. Maple worktops come somewhere
between the light and dark tones, to add a
touch of natural texture. The bold stripes of
the Roman blind add graphic pattern and give
the room a feeling of height.

▲ A large kitchen can take strong colour, and there's no more powerful combination than deep raspberry red and sharp yellow. Here the red dominates, used for both paintwork and tiles to entirely cover the walls, while the units and chair were given a coat of yellow paint that tones with the wood colour of the table and bench. Black accents add a smart touch, and the large floor area claims its own share of the attention with a jazzy chequer-board design.

▶ The colours of fresh ripe fruit promote a feeling of vitality, so try zesty citrus shades to invigorate and energize in your kitchen. Primary colours work best on a backdrop of white, so add areas of colour to a white wall or use just a few white tiles to break up coloured ones. Try not to be too regimental or symmetrical – uneven shapes and patterns will stimulate and give you a kick-start on bleary-eyed mornings. Furniture should be unfussy yet fun.

◀ Units painted in deep red contrast with tongue-and-groove panelling in cool cream and a light beech worktop to create this colourful interpretation of a Shaker-style kitchen. The unpainted wooden peg rail is a typical feature of Shaker rooms, and its pegs are echoed by the simple dowelling knobs on the wall units above. Baskets and other woven accessories reinforce the Shaker theme, the deep red units forming a dramatic backdrop for their natural textures.

▲ Deep maroon paintwork smartens up a small kitchen without compromising the feeling of space; the plain white walls reflect natural light from the window. The butler's sink and wooden worktops and door knobs give a nod to country style, while the sleek shimmer of chrome appliances is highlighted against the dark colour of the units. The stark contrast between the white and maroon is softened by the row of handmade cream tiles surrounding the worktop.

▶ White walls and stainless steel fittings and appliances bounce light around in this sleek, modern kitchen, and pale maple flooring emphasizes the feeling of space. But although colour is confined to the window treatments, table runner and skirtings, it is a key feature of the room, the hot pinks and magentas jumping out from a sea of white. These boldly clashing shades were inspired by Indian saris, and the shiny silk fabrics go well with the gleaming steel.

▶ If you like laid-back simplicity, bring a touch of New England style to your home. Warm wood and checked fabrics team up for a look that's perfect for relaxed dining. The colour palette majors on blue, red and white. For a contemporary interpretation of the style, set your furniture against a deep purple-blue background and paint your floorboards white.

Dining rooms

◀ Blue and green often make perfect partners, even if the shades used are very different in tone. In this colourful diner, walls in delicate lime green add a refreshing feel alongside a dresser covered in a robust ultramarine blue. The top of the walls and the ceiling are painted in white to add a feeling of space and height to the room. The full-length curtains repeat the bold blue of the dresser, and also echo the green and white in their floral design.

▲ A zingy apple green means breakfast time is anything but boring in this wide-awake room. More vibrant, fruity shades are featured in the tablecloth, where a bright red colour tones with yellow and orange in bold checks. The narrow green stripes that outline the checks echo the wall colour. The rich, natural tones of the unpainted woodwork and matching wooden furniture offset the walls at the same time as blending with the warmer colours.

▲ Get conversation buzzing around your dinner table with a sharply contrasting scheme of lime green and deep orange, using them on different walls and to mark out features such as fireplaces. The door is painted in soft green, adding another eye-catching colour to a background that begs to be noticed. In the foreground, the table also makes a bid for attention, with a zappy PVC covering in a jade green check and legs sporting matching paintwork.

▶ Even the tiniest of eating areas can benefit from a colour makeover. The simple table was given the designer look with a coat of vibrant blue paint and a contrasting lime green border. The blue was applied first all over the tabletop and left to dry, then the border was masked off with tape before being painted. As a fun touch, the wooden chairs were decorated in two different colours. With bright yellow as the backdrop, this slick paintwork is sure to cheer up mealtimes.

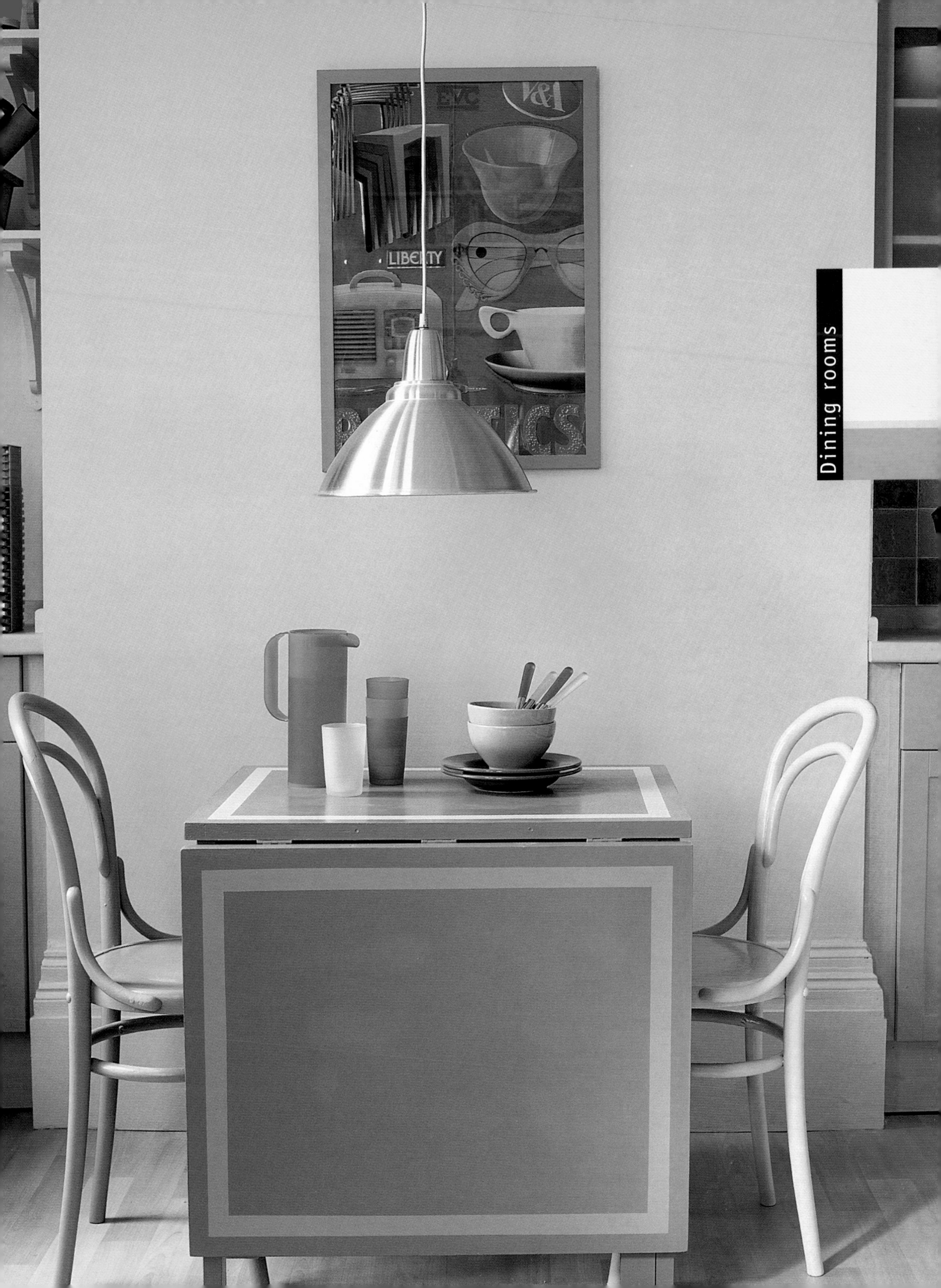
LIBERTY

◀ Mix crisp white with salad greens for a look that's cool as a cucumber. Bright green walls keep their freshness when you team them with plenty of clean white – as in the painted furniture and window frames. A gleaming wood floor and accents of shiny metal enhance the refreshing feel, with no other colours to muddy the effect. The checks of the window blind and tie-on chair covers add a light country look to the simple two-colour scheme.

▲ If you hanker after an air of faded grandeur, what better way to create it than with ice-cool pastels and elegant white-painted furniture? Choose barely-there blues and smoky greys, keeping them pale throughout the room, and team with lots of sparkling crystal and candles to set the mood. For true French château style, gather swathes of fabric patterned with flowers and leaves into generous sweeping drapes, and hold them back with huge tassel tiebacks.

◀ Surrounded by plain cream and white decor, this dining area in a spacious converted barn is marked out by the bright yellow rug, which complements the wood flooring while adding a touch of comfort underfoot. With its lofty roof, this is a space for casual entertaining rather than intimate dining, a point emphasized by the blue garden-style chairs and makeshift table – two sheets of green-painted MDF balanced on trestles.

▲ With its dark wood floor, this dining area needed a light wall colour to lift the gloom and add a feeling of space. So two shades of soft taupe were chosen, one for the main part of the walls and a darker shade to highlight the alcove. The neutral theme continues with chair covers made from plain creamy calico and a tablecloth in grey and white, but it's the flashes of orange in the curtains, seat cushions and tableware that give the scheme its bright and cheerful feel.

▶ Dramatically patterned wallpaper with a traditional *toile de Jouy* design gives this dining room a smart classical look that suits the period-style fireplace and wood-panelled walls. The black and white fireplace continues the monochrome theme, while the lower walls add a splash of colour to lift the scheme. Black and white works well with just about any hue – here cool blue introduces a contemporary touch, with lilac and aqua tableware adding further spots of colour.

▲ The collection of brightly coloured artwork is the focal point of this dining room, and the two rows of pictures are shown off to stunning effect against the pale ochre wall colour. Softer and more sociable than cream or white, this shade also harmonizes with the warm orange tones of the cherrywood dining table and terracotta floor tiles. The huge cactus plant in its woven pot adds a splash of green as well as a striking finishing touch.

▲ Cool cream walls and furniture in warm wood tones may provide all the colour you need to feel comfortable in your dining room, but if you sometimes get the yen for a little bit more, then why not store away a secret colour fix inside your cupboards or wall units? A combination of vivid fuchsia pink and royal blue is revealed when these doors open, but any bright colours would create similar impact against such a plain background.

◀ A Tuscan look was the aim in this dining room, where the sun-baked atmosphere of Italy has been recreated with a warm ochre scumble glaze on the walls. The earthy colour scheme continues with the furniture and table settings, which are rich in rustic texture. Rattan chairs and a table made of reclaimed pine are teamed with hemp table mats and decorative terracotta pots containing twig balls. Sunlight filters through wooden slatted blinds.

▲ If you've a taste for the exotic, bring the hot spicy colours of India to your table. A richly embroidered scarlet sari serving as a tablecloth is piled with gold and silver-edged tableware, shiny pitchers and jewel-encrusted goblets. Dark wood furniture is in keeping with this theme, especially if it has fretwork panels or carved detailing. To offset the glitzy table setting, choose a soft neutral for the walls, such as this mushroom shade.

125

▲ Pink and green is one of nature's favourite pairings. Deep leafy greens take away the sugary edge from petal-pink walls, while a sheer blind in white and a lighter green makes the most of the natural light that streams through the window. The creamy white table and dresser contrast with the sombre green of the Lloyd Loom chairs. Deeper tones of pink are included in the cushions that brighten up the chairs, and in the plum-coloured tableware.

▶ Deep colours make for an intimate air in a dining room, and plum is an excellent choice if you do a lot of evening entertaining. Used in its full intensity on the walls, this rich shade creates a warm and stimulating atmosphere, especially when teamed with deep-toned wood flooring and dark curtains. Add touches of white to highlight the depth of colour, but don't overdo them. Extend the comfort factor to the table with a coloured runner and plushy seat cushions in red and plum.

◀ Take a shine to silver for a sleek modern dining room that looks like a million dollars. Set the scene with shimmering metallic-effect wallpapers with subtle designs, then add a silver wall border and spray inexpensive chairs with metallic paint. Accessories with clean lines and simple curvy shapes add a little extra shimmer. To warm up a silver scheme, include hints of soft pink and lilac. The canvas covered in lilac fabric adds colour above eye level.

▲ Impact is the keynote in this room that can't fail to catch the eye. Shocking pink is a bold but flattering colour to use for a dining area as it brings a healthy glow to people's faces as they sit around the table. To prevent it from overwhelming, the ceiling and walls above the picture rail are painted white, which also creates a dazzling contrast. Cow-print chair covers add a quirky touch, while a sober grey carpet 'grounds' the vibrant scheme.

▶ For a look that's totally up-to-date, choose one intense colour and introduce a mix of different shades. This bedroom layers bold blues with aqua, indigo and turquoise, adding splashes of white to tone them down. The wall behind the bed is painted in horizontal stripes of many different shades, graduating from the darkest blue at floor level.

Bedrooms

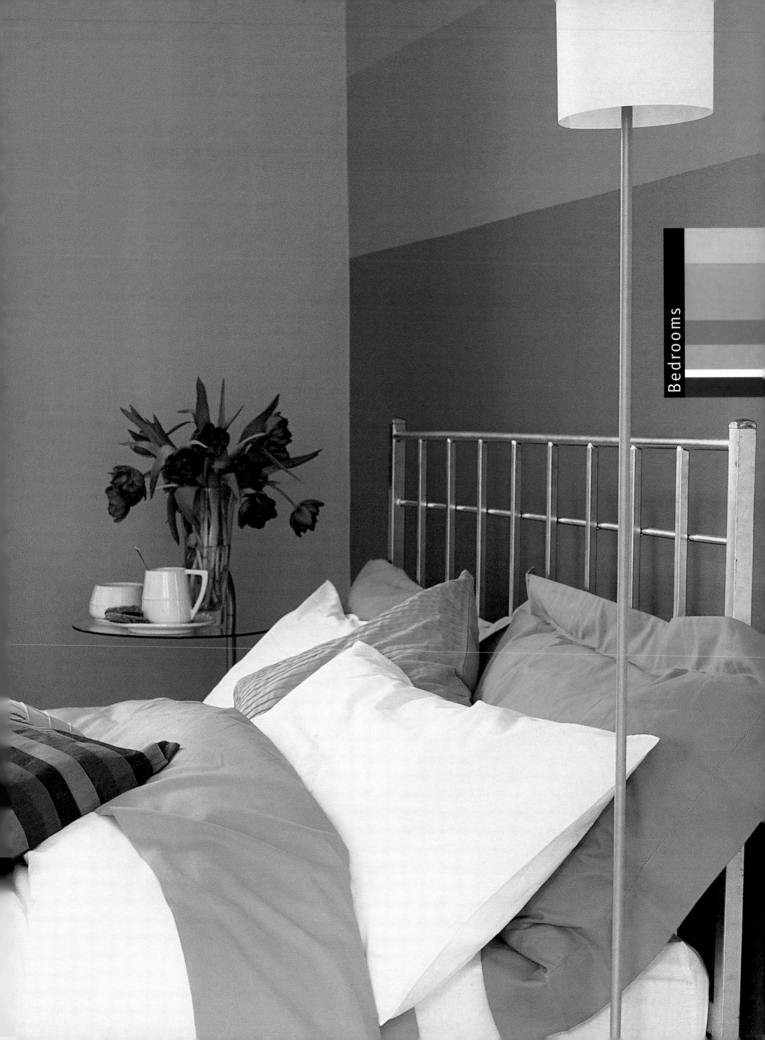

Bedrooms

◀ Often it's the way colours are used rather than the shades themselves that gives a scheme its unique character. A simple combination of blue and white creates this distinctive marquee-style effect, with the walls covered in stripes. Applied as a light wash, they look more delicate than if painted in solid colour, and are repeated on the headboard and footboard of the bed. Blue glass accessories provide a more intense dose of colour.

▲ Without being as obviously glitzy as gold, pewter and silver can help to create a glamorous bedroom. Complement the metallic accessories and fabrics with muted blues and dusky greys for a calming but subtly seductive atmosphere. Glistening voile panels and piles of glimmering silk and velvet cushions add to the luxurious look, while squares of silver leaf applied to the painted mirror frame are the perfect finishing touch.

◀ Cool blue and silver complemented by tangy orange create a vibrant playing environment for two boys. Their wish for an outer-space theme inspired the silver furnishings, with the splattered paint effect on the walls giving the illusion of a night sky. Using white emulsion and a blue several shades darker than the wall, it was applied by dipping a brush in a little paint and hitting a piece of wood against the handle, directing the paint at the wall.

▲ Many focus on the walls when considering using colour, but in this room they remain white amid the almost childlike medley of stimulating shades. Vivid blue makes a feature of the bed, while the darker background of the artwork beside it contrasts with golden yellow curtains. Even the door gets the colour treatment, painted in stunning pink with a green handle. All these are colours picked out from the rainbow checks of the bedspread.

▲ A world away from Japan, oriental minimalism finds a home in an attic bedroom. The walls were painted with cream emulsion then washed in a sandy shade, using a soft brush. When dry, a sander was run over them to give the look of rice paper. The floorboards were painted with two shades of grey for a gentle colour mix that tones with the soft blue of the bedcover. Throws and cushions in rich colours and textures add a sensual touch.

▶ Get comfortable with the natural look by mixing shades of coffee, caramel and cream. Squares painted on the fireplace wall show off this tonal variation, which is repeated in the cushions, pillows and bedlinen. A knitted throw and cushion add an element of texture to the subtle mix. A masculine mood is evoked by the smartly striped pillows, geometric furniture and hardwood window blind, as well as the accents of black introduced in accessories.

▲ Blocks of strong colour add up to a strikingly simple scheme which relies on the contrasts between them for its success. As complementary colours, the apple green and raspberry pink intensify each other to give full impact, while the blue, although a cool contrast, is deep enough to hold its own with these vivid shades. Painting the radiator to match the walls makes it blend in, without interrupting the all-encompassing colour.

▲ Evoke a colonial feel with exotic lime-green paint, a bed shrouded in mosquito netting and sheer, softly draped curtains in white muslin. Natural wood goes well with this look, so leave the window frames and other woodwork unpainted and choose traditional-style dark wood furniture. Ethnic prints reinforce the theme further – stick to light neutral colours for the bedcoverings so as not to detract from the freshness of the green.

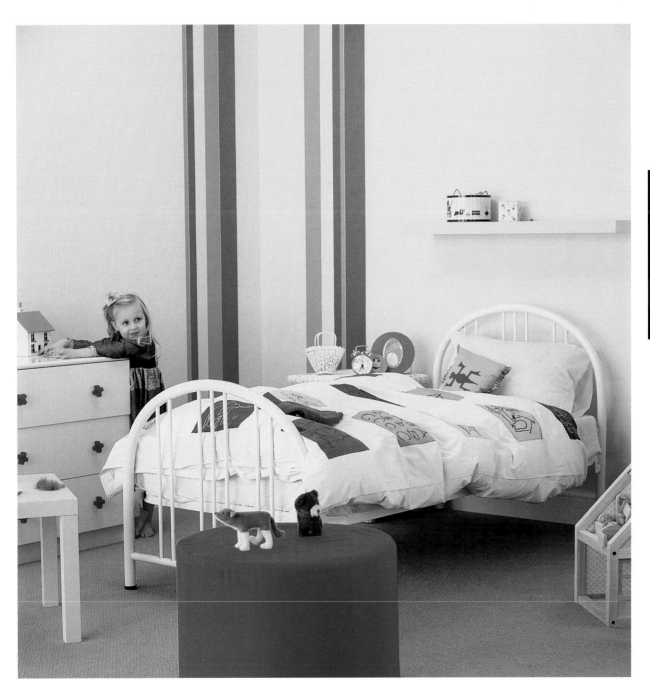

◄ A refreshing contemporary green brings this high-ceilinged Victorian room into the twenty-first century, with the picture rail and fire surround picked out in clean white. The bedcover continues the look with soft shades of lilac and green, which harmonize with the wall colour to create a gentle, easy-going atmosphere. The plain-painted chimney breast makes an ideal display space for the pair of collages, which add eye-catching colour.

▲ A child's room is one place in the house where you can afford to go wild with colour. This bright bedroom contains all the colours of the rainbow, with dynamic stripes in contrasting contemporary shades adding a touch of fun to the sunshine-yellow walls. The mix of colours is repeated in the squares on the duvet cover, which stand out against the white background. The blue carpet provides a cool base for the glowing reds and yellows.

◀ Strong cranberry red dominates this room to create a dramatic contemporary scheme. Such a hot colour will make any room feel smaller, so here it is used with two shades of pink, to offset the effect a little. Fading the bands of colour from deep red through to palest pink leads the eye up to the top of the walls, making the room seem taller. Pure white helps to lighten the mood and adds graphic impact, while the striking rose print and gingham pillowcases introduce an element of pattern.

Bedrooms

▲ Painting a tiny boxroom bright pink is a brave move, but this warm, rosy shade has created a pretty bedroom for a little girl. The white ceiling, straw-coloured carpet and cream curtains prevent the pink from being too overpowering, even though it has been used extensively, to cover the cupboard doors, skirtings and radiators as well as the walls. The pine bed was revamped with chalk-coloured gloss, then roses were painted on.

▶ Subtle glamour goes down well with teenage girls, and soft lilac is just the colour to create a cool, contemporary backdrop. With simple furniture and plenty of plain white as a light contrast, they are free to add a bit of glitz without overdoing things. Here it comes from accessories such as the heart-shaped mirror and plush purple cushion. Modern patterns with strong shapes or abstract designs add a sophisticated touch.

◀ For a soothing scheme with a sensuous atmosphere, combine twilight shades of lilac with deep, dark plum and aubergine, blending them with gentle pinks, paler mauves and a little pure white to soften the intensity of the scheme. To up the comfort factor, introduce luxurious textures such as velvet and fake fur. The curvy side table, painted in a vivid fuchsia pink, adds a lively accent to offset the backdrop of sultry shades.

▲ This is the stuff of fairy-tales, with a fully dressed four-poster highlighted against a dreamy shade of lilac. The wall colour is continued on the ceiling, while the skirtings are painted in a darker purple and the floor is covered with a toning grey carpet. Sticking to soft shades for the background decor ensures that the white drapes and bedlinen take centrestage. The oriental hanging and pictures provide original finishing touches.

▲ Give yourself a gentle start to the day by waking up to the prettiest of florals in the softest of pastel shades. Tiny sprig prints share the bed with big blooms, all on a background of crisp white. Pink is the link colour for this flower garden of fabrics, featuring in the curtains, pillows and bedlinen, so is also a natural choice for the walls. The chair adds a more intense shade to the light-toned scheme, picking up on the colour of the largest roses.

▶ For a bedroom full of springtime freshness, use leafy greens to sharpen the prettiness of blossom pinks and lilacs. Use the lightest green on the walls, then add zingier shades as accents. Choose bedding and cushions in delicate tones of lilac, lavender and rose, and keep bed drapes sheer – this canopy is made of subtly patterned voile. Add deeper colour only in small amounts, as in the purple rug and cushion, to give the scheme depth.

▶ Bring a sophisticated sheen to bathtime with the gleam of copper. Metallic paint gives this roll-top tub its opulent glow, while the shelves are edged with copper leaf. The flooring is a copper lookalike. Sage green and cream provide the perfect understated backdrop, and grey towels add accent colour without stealing the spotlight from the glamorous copper finishes.

Bathrooms

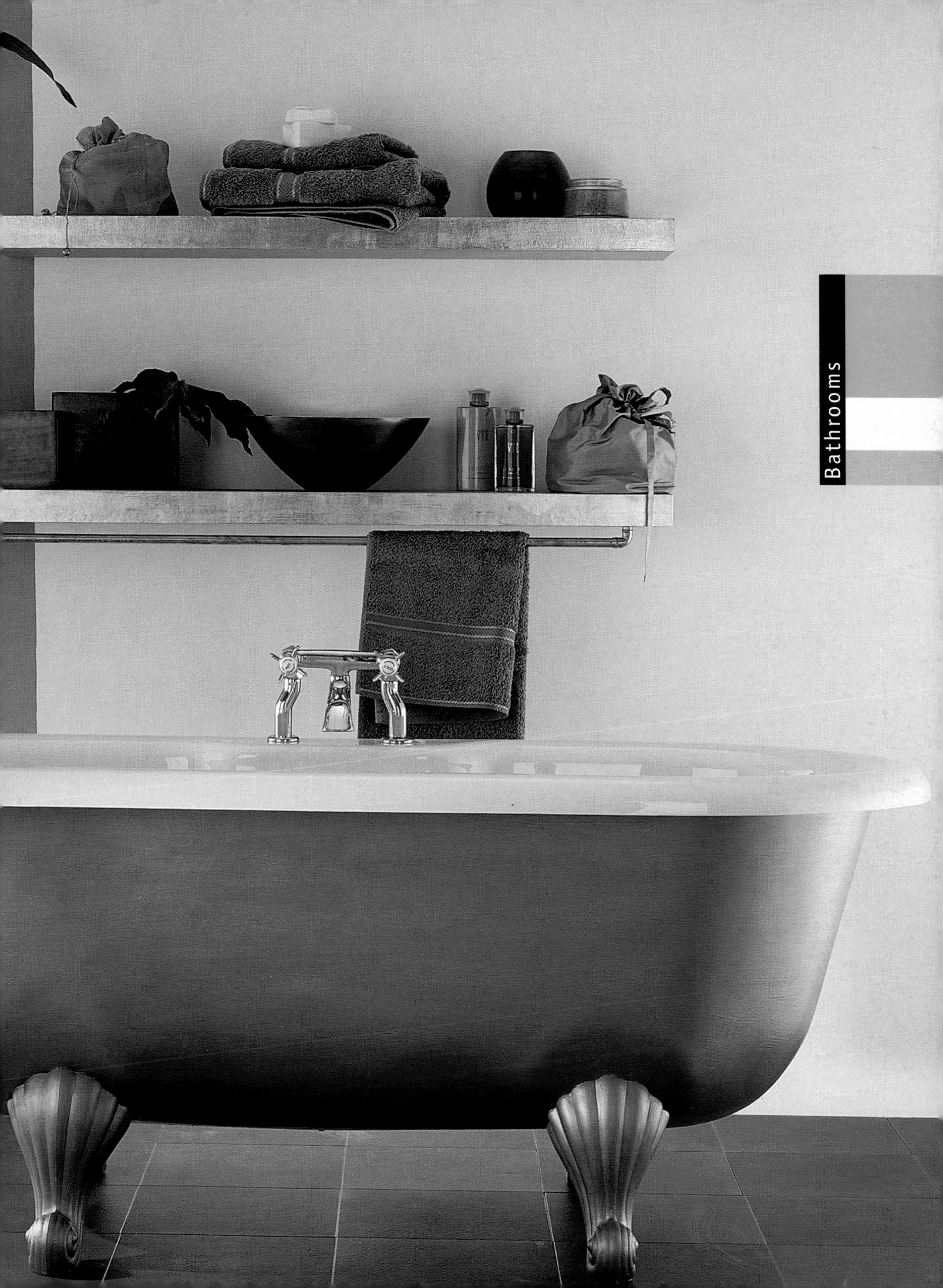

◄ Using light colours throughout will add a sense of space to the smallest bathroom. Too much white can give a clinical feel, but cream creates a clean look that's easier to live with. Stick to white for the suite, though; not only is a white suite more versatile but it also provides a crisp contrast for the cream, giving it a contemporary edge. Wood panelling has a warmer feel than tiles, while the carved dark wood cabinet and picture frame add character.

▲ Spicy colours warm up this mainly cream scheme, with yellow ochre paintwork on the basin and loo housing, and orange and cream tiles alternating to make a subtle splashback. A blind in crisp ginger and white ticking brightens up the window. Baskets and wooden accessories work with the earthy colours to create a natural feel. The framed picture, made from handmade paper and willow cane, adds an ethnic touch as well as extra colour.

▲ Although light shades give the illusion of space, deep colours can also work wonders in small bathrooms, adding drama and warmth. Use them plain rather than patterned, and stick to simple styling. In this room with more than a hint of oriental style, rose pink, honey-coloured wood and buff mosaic create a welcoming mix. The pink is balanced by the pale wood and lighter tiles, and boxing in the bath and basin ensures clean lines.

▶ Earthy shades turn up the heat in this chilly high-ceilinged room in a way that draws attention to and makes the most of its original features – the picture rail and ornate coving. Three colours have been used: a deep red on the main part of the walls, a slightly darker shade on the picture rail and a pale yellow between the rail and coving. The warm caramel tones of the wood flooring and loo seat complement the wall colours.

◄ This daring scheme shows how two complementary colours – yellow and purple – bring out the best in each other. When combining two strong colours, keep the deeper one for the lower part of the room. It 'grounds' the scheme, while the brighter shade keeps the atmosphere airy. Continue the wall colours over shelves and skirtings. A scheme of two bold colours needs touches of a third for balance; here accents of sharp green do the job.

▲ If you can't decide which colour to go for, try them all together! Bright yellow, turquoise and lilac used cheek by jowl in the same small area might sound like a recipe for disaster, but they bring a fun, lively look to this bathroom. More colour is included as accents – in the deep pink and orange towels and the green candles in both light and dark tones. The flowers of the shower curtain echo the lilac and turquoise wall colours.

157

▲ Crisp and clean, this bathroom shows how furniture and fittings can be as important as colour in setting the scene. The sleek metal cabinet and stainless steel bath panelling give the scheme its modern, clinical, feel. These reflective surfaces also earn their keep in a small space by bouncing light around the room. The cool blue on the walls provides just enough colour to make the look livable, while splashes of red energize the scheme.

▶ Blues and aquas, reminiscent of sea and sky, are popular choices for bathrooms. It's easy to see why, as they're real feelgood hues. This scheme brings together a number of harmonising shades – from watery aquas to rich turquoise – to create a look that's enrichingly colourful but also deeply relaxing. Small amounts of pure white, in the bathroom fittings and on the skirting board, provide a clean contrast for the floor-to-ceiling colour.

◀ Contrast is the name of the game in this bright and breezy bathroom where deep pink and sparkling white stand out against a sea of cool blue. The vertical panels of pink and white act like stripes, leading the eye upwards and adding height to the room. They also draw together the basin, shelves and mirror to make an eye-catching feature of the wall space between the bath and loo. The pink is repeated on the woodwork of the window frame.

▲ Deep Mediterranean blue is a bold choice for this bathroom. An electrifying contrast comes from accents of bright pink, which were inspired by the pink plastic bath toy. White-painted floorboards provide a light base for the strong colours, while the clean white of the bath and the simple, sheer curtains freshen up things further. Pink and white are woven together in the chair and linen basket, perfect accessories for the scheme.

▲ The panel of bright-blue tiles is the attention-grabbing feature in this room, where they run from the window to the basin to form a vibrant block of colour in contrast to the white suite. The flooring is a sparkly vinyl in a much lighter blue. Painting the walls pale blue as well might have made the small dark room feel too cold, so they have been given a coat of mint green, which lifts the scheme. The wooden Venetian blind is a matching shade.

▶ Pale watery blues cover all paintable surfaces to lighten even the gloomiest areas of this large but awkwardly shaped bathroom. The lines of the wood panelling on the walls and bath surround introduce an element of pattern to the plain scheme, while the high wall shelf brings a sense of proportion to the high-ceilinged room. Small rectangles of floral fabric, displayed in frames along the shelf, add a further decorative touch.

◀ For a look that's light but soothing, soft aqua green is the answer. It brings a refreshing, spacious feel to this small bathroom, driving out dinginess while still filling the room with colour. The key to creating a restful scheme is combining harmonious hues or different tones of one colour. The bath is painted a darker green, while silvery blue slate floor tiles and splashback tiles in watery greens and greys harmonize with the aqua paintwork.

▲ With jade-green louvred shutters and walls painted in a deep shade of terracotta, this small bathroom recreates the feel of an old Italian villa. The MDF bath panelling has been scumble-glazed to give the look of a beach hut weathered by brine and breeze, and is thrown into relief by the chocolate-brown flooring. The white suite and tiles, which are set diagonally for extra interest, provide the necessary light contrast for all these dark, moody tones.

▲ Black and white is not an easy combination to live with in rooms where you spend a lot of time, but in a bathroom it can look smart and striking, and is a classic choice if you want a more hard-edged, masculine style. Big chequerboard tiles and black rubber flooring make a dramatic statement. To slightly alleviate the starkness of the monochrome scheme, the bath is painted chocolate brown and the upper walls are in a light mustard.

▶ This striking modern bathroom combines the hard-edged industrial style of galvanised metal with a lush grass green on the walls. The bath panels and splashback are covered in pre-weathered zinc titanium alloy. Despite all the metal, the look has an essentially natural character, which is enhanced by the sisal-effect flooring and wicker chair. Leafy pot plants in brighter greens join with the stunning wall colour to suggest a tropical feel.